Baby animals in mountain habitats

Bobbie Kalman

🌳 Crabtree Publishing Company

www.crabtreebooks.com

The Habitats of Baby Animals

Created by Bobbie Kalman

Dedicated by Samara Parent
For my nephew Elliott (Little 'E')
Have fun discovering nature in all its beauty! Love, Aunty Samara

**Author and
Editor-in-Chief**
Bobbie Kalman

Editors
Kathy Middleton
Crystal Sikkens

Design
Bobbie Kalman
Katherine Berti
Samantha Crabtree
(front cover)

Photo research
Bobbie Kalman

Print and production coordinator
Katherine Berti

Prepress technician
Katherine Berti

Illustrations
Barbara Bedell: pages 6 (leaves), 7 (pine cone)
Katherine Berti: pages 6–7

Photographs
BigStockPhoto: pages 9 (top), 24 (top right)
Dreamstime: pages 13, 21 (top), 24 (bottom right)
iStockphoto: pages 10 (bottom left), 19 (top),
     23 (bottom left), 24 (food chain-bottom left)
Photos.com: page 12
Wikipedia/NPS/John Good: page 11 (top right)
Other photographs by Shutterstock

Library and Archives Canada Cataloguing in Publication

Kalman, Bobbie, 1947-
    Baby animals in mountain habitats / Bobbie Kalman.

(The habitats of baby animals)
Includes index.
Issued also in electronic format.
ISBN 978-0-7787-7728-1 (bound).--ISBN 978-0-7787-7741-0 (pbk.)

    1. Mountain animals--Infancy--Juvenile literature. 2. Mountain
ecology--Juvenile literature. I. Title. II. Series: Kalman, Bobbie, 1947- .
Habitats of baby animals.

QL113.K34 2011   j591.3'909143   C2010-907520-X

Library of Congress Cataloging-in-Publication Data

Kalman, Bobbie.
 Baby animals in mountain habitats / Bobbie Kalman.
     p. cm. -- (The habitats of baby animals)
 Includes index.
 ISBN 978-0-7787-7741-0 (pbk. : alk. paper) -- ISBN 978-0-7787-7728-1
(reinforced library binding : alk. paper) -- ISBN 978-1-4271-9603-3 (electronic
(pdf))
 1. Mountain animals--Infancy--Juvenile literature. 2. Mountain animals--
Ecology--Juvenile literature. I. Title.
 QL113.K35 2011
 591.75'3--dc22

                                        2010047919

Crabtree Publishing Company
www.crabtreebooks.com   1-800-387-7650

Printed in China/022011/RG20101116

**Published in Canada
Crabtree Publishing**
616 Welland Ave.
St. Catharines, Ontario
L2M 5V6

**Published in the United States
Crabtree Publishing**
PMB 59051
350 Fifth Avenue, 59th Floor
New York, New York 10118

**Published in the United Kingdom
Crabtree Publishing**
Maritime House
Basin Road North, Hove
BN41 1WR

**Published in Australia
Crabtree Publishing**
386 Mt. Alexander Rd.
Ascot Vale (Melbourne)
VIC 3032

What is in this book?

What is a habitat?

A **habitat** is a place in nature. Plants and animals live in habitats. They are **living things**. Living things grow, change, and make new living things. Plants make new plants, and animals make babies. These baby mountain goats are living things.

*Young mountain goats are called **kids**.*

Living and non-living

Habitats are made up of living and **non-living things**. Air, sunshine, rocks, soil, and water are non-living things. Living things need non-living things. They also need other living things. Living things find the things they need in their habitats.

Mountain habitats

Mountains are areas of rocky land that rise high above the ground. Most mountains have steep sides. Steep sides rise almost straight up from the ground. There are different habitats on mountains. Trees and other plants grow at the bottom of mountains. At the top of mountains are habitats called **alpine tundras**. There are no trees in alpine tundras.

*Different plants grow on different parts of mountains. The weather at the bottom of a mountain is warmer than it is at the top. Flowers and **forests** can grow here. A forest is an area with many trees.*

Trees stop growing near the top of mountains. The winds are too strong. Strong winds would blow the trees down. The area where trees stop growing is called the **tree line**.

conifers

Conifers grow higher up on mountains. Conifers are trees with cones and thin leaves that look like needles.

cone

Homes in habitats

Some animal mothers keep their babies safe in **dens**, or homes. They find many places to hide their babies between and under mountain rocks. This mother red fox hides her kit in a den under some big rocks.

These coyote pups live inside a rock den on a mountainside.

*Marmots dig **burrows**, or tunnels, under rocks. This marmot mother and baby live in a burrow under the rocks behind them. They sleep there all winter.*

Mountain babies

Some of the animals that live on mountains are ground squirrels, mountain lions, mountain goats, bighorn sheep, coyotes, wolves, red foxes, marmots, and pikas. What are the babies of these animals called?

mountain lion cub (also cougar cub)

ground squirrel pup

baby pika

red fox kit

wolf pup

coyote pup

bighorn
lamb

marmot pup

mountain
goat kid

Mothers and babies

All the babies on pages 10 and 11 are **mammals**. Mammals are animals with hair or fur. Mammal babies are born live. Mammal mothers look after their babies after the babies are born. They keep them safe and teach them how to hunt or find food.

This mountain lion mother takes good care of her cubs. She keeps them in a den under some rocks and moves them often to keep them safe.

After their babies are born, mammal mothers feed them milk from their bodies. Drinking mother's milk is called **nursing**. Three of these wolf pups are nursing.

13

Climbing with hoofs

Mountain animals are suited to climbing mountains. Some, such as bighorn sheep and mountain goats, have **hoofs**. Hoofs are hard toes. Hoofs with two toes help mountain animals grip rocks. Hoofed mountain animals are able to climb steep rocks to escape **predators** such as coyotes, wolves, and cougars. Predators are animals that hunt and eat other animals.

This mountain goat kid uses its hoofs to climb a very high and steep mountain.

This bighorn sheep family had no trouble climbing on these steep rocks. They have hoofs!

15

Mountain rodents

Rodents are mammals with four front teeth that never stop growing. Marmots, ground squirrels, mice, and chipmunks are rodents that live in mountain habitats. Many kinds of predators, such as foxes, coyotes, and mountain lions, eat rodents.

Ground squirrels look like chipmunks, but they do not have stripes on their heads. They live in burrows and eat mainly plants. They spend very little time in trees.

A marmot is a kind of ground squirrel. Marmots live in underground burrows with their families. During the day, they come above ground to eat grasses, berries, roots, and flowers. They sleep through the winter in their burrows.

Alpine chipmunks live on mountains. They have brown foreheads with three white stripes on their cheeks. They have four stripes on their backs.

Eating plants

Many animals that live on mountains eat plants. Animals that feed mainly on plants are called **herbivores**. Mountain goats, bighorn sheep, marmots, ground squirrels, rabbits, and pikas are herbivores. They eat the grasses, flowers, and weeds that grow on the sides of mountains.

This marmot is munching on some mountain flowers.

Pikas belong to the rabbit family. They eat grasses and flowers, just as rabbits do.

This mountain goat kid finds plenty of grasses to eat on the lower parts of mountains.

Mountain carnivores

Carnivores are animals that eat other animals. Red foxes, coyotes, cougars, and wolves are carnivores that live on mountains. Birds such as eagles and hawks fly above mountain habitats looking for animals to eat.

bald eagle

This wolf pup is learning what meat tastes like from its mother's mouth. The mother brings up food from her stomach, and the pup eats it. A pup licks its mother's mouth to let her know that it is hungry for meat.

Coyotes hunt mountain goats, marmots, rabbits, birds, and ground squirrels. This young coyote is playing outside its den, but it will soon start hunting.

*This red fox kit is learning to hunt from its mother. It will hunt pikas, rabbits, and mice. It will also eat eggs, insects, and plants when it cannot find animals to hunt. Foxes are animals called **omnivores**. Omnivores eat both plants and animals.*

What is a food chain?

Animals need **energy**, or power. They need energy to breathe, move, grow, and stay alive. They get their energy from eating other living things. A **food chain** is the passing of energy from one living thing to another. When an animal eats a plant, and another animal eats that animal, there is a food chain.